Thrall

Books by Natasha Trethewey

Thrall

POEMS

Natasha Trethewey

Mariner Books
Houghton Mifflin Harcourt
Boston   New York

First Mariner Books edition 2015

Copyright © 2012 by Natasha Trethewey

For information about permission to reproduce selections from this book, write to Permissions, Houghton Mifflin Harcourt Publishing Company, 215 Park Avenue South, New York, New York 10003.

www.hmhco.com

Library of Congress Cataloging-in-Publication Data
Trethewey, Natasha D., date.
Thrall : poems / Natasha Trethewey.
p. cm.
ISBN 978-0-547-57160-7   ISBN 978-0-544-58620-8 (pbk.)
I. Title.
PS3570.R433T47 2012
811'.54—dc23
2012017321

Book design by Greta D. Sibley
Printed in the United States of America
DOC 10 9 8 7 6 5 4 3 2 1

To my father

What is love?

One name for it is knowledge.

    — *Robert Penn Warren*

After such knowledge, what forgiveness?

    — *T. S. Eliot*

Contents

Thrall

Elegy

For my father

I think by now the river must be thick
    with salmon. Late August, I imagine it

as it was that morning: drizzle needling
    the surface, mist at the banks like a net

settling around us — everything damp
    and shining. That morning, awkward

and heavy in our hip waders, we stalked
    into the current and found our places —

you upstream a few yards and out
    far deeper. You must remember how

the river seeped in over your boots
    and you grew heavier with that defeat.

All day I kept turning to watch you, how
    first you mimed our guide's casting

then cast your invisible line, slicing the sky

    between us; and later, rod in hand, how

you tried — again and again — to find

    that perfect arc, flight of an insect

skimming the river's surface. Perhaps

    you recall I cast my line and reeled in

two small trout we could not keep.

    Because I had to release them, I confess,

I thought about the past — working

    the hooks loose, the fish writhing

in my hands, each one slipping away

    before I could let go. I can tell you now

that I tried to take it all in, record it

    for an elegy I'd write — one day —

when the time came. Your daughter,

    I was that ruthless. What does it matter

if I tell you I *learned* to be? You kept casting

    your line, and when it did not come back

empty, it was tangled with mine. Some nights,

    dreaming, I step again into the small boat

that carried us out and watch the bank receding —

    my back to where I know we are headed.

Miracle of the Black Leg

*Pictorial representations of the physician-saints Cosmas and
Damian and the myth of the miracle transplant — black donor,
white recipient — date back to the mid-fourteenth century,
appearing much later than written versions of the story.*

1.

Always, the dark body hewn asunder; always

    one man is healed, his sick limb replaced,

placed in the other man's grave: the white leg

    buried beside the corpse or attached as if

it were always there. If not for the dark appendage

    you might miss the story beneath this story —

what remains each time the myth changes: how,

    in one version, the doctors harvest the leg

from a man, four days dead, in his tomb at the church

    of a martyr, or — in another — desecrate a body

fresh in the graveyard at Saint Peter in Chains:

    there was buried just today an Ethiopian.

Even now, it stays with us: when we mean to uncover

    the truth, we dig, say *unearth.*

dig the story out of the grave

Emblematic in paint, a signifier of the body's lacuna,

    the black leg is at once a grafted narrative,

a redacted line of text, and in this scene a dark stocking

    pulled above the knee. Here the patient is sleeping,

his head at rest in his hand. Beatific, he looks as if

    he'll wake from a dream. On the floor

beside the bed, a dead *Moor* — hands crossed at the groin,

    the swapped limb white and rotting, fused in place.

And in the corner, a question: poised as if to speak

    the syntax of sloughing, a snake's curved form.

It emerges from the mouth of a boy like a tongue — slippery

    and rooted in the body as knowledge. For centuries

this is how the myth repeats: the miracle — in words

    or wood or paint — is a record of thought.

[handwritten margin note: symbolic of dispensibility of dead man]

[handwritten margin note: this painter shows the black man as sub human by painting him as just a dead body]

See how the story changes: in one painting

the *Ethiop* is merely a body, featureless in a coffin,

so black he has no face. In another, the patient —

at the top of the frame — seems to writhe in pain,

the black leg grafted to his thigh. Below him

a mirror of suffering: the *blackamoor* —

his body a fragment — arched across the doctor's lap

as if dying from his wound. If not immanence,

the soul's bright anchor — blood passed from one

to the other — what knowledge haunts each body,

what history, what phantom ache? One man always

low, in a grave or on the ground, the other

up high, closer to heaven; one man always diseased,

the other a body in service, plundered.

[handwritten left margin: being black renders him inhuman]

[handwritten right margin: this painter passes judgement by making both men look pained]

4.

Both men are alive in Villoldo's carving.

In twinned relief, they hold the same posture,

the same pained face, each man reaching to touch

his left leg. The black man, on the floor,

holds his stump. Above him, the doctor restrains

the patient's arm as if to prevent him touching

the dark amendment of flesh. How not to see it —

the men bound one to the other, symbiotic —

one man rendered expendable, the other worthy

of this sacrifice? In version after version, even

when the *Ethiopian* isn't there, the leg is a stand-in,

a black modifier against the white body,

a piece cut off — as in the origin of the word *comma:*

caesura in a story that's still being written.

On Captivity

> Being all Stripped as Naked as We were Born, and endeavoring
> to hide our Nakedness, these Cannaballs took [our] Books, and
> tearing out the Leaves would give each of us a Leaf to cover us . . .
> — *Jonathan Dickinson, 1699*

At the hands now

    of their captors, those

        they've named *savages,*

    do they say the word itself

savagely — hissing

*captors make
them savages
by taking their clothes*

clothes = civilization

that first letter,

    the serpent's image

        releasing

    thought into speech?

For them now

*knowledge of
good + evil*

*white people?
captives.*

everything is flesh

    as if their thoughts, made

        suddenly corporeal,

    reveal even more

their nakedness —

*using words to
reclaim their
humanity*

knowlege clothing

knowlege = protection

the shame of it:

    their bodies rendered

        plain as the natives' —

    homely and pale,   *human as*

                            captive

their ordinary sex,

when everything is stripped
away they realize knowlege

the secret illicit hairs

    that do not (cannot)

        cover enough.

    Naked as newborns,

this is how they are brought

to knowledge. Adam and Eve   *but what's inside*

    in the New World,   *their minds keeps*

        they have only the Bible *them human*

    to cover them. Think of it:

a woman holding before her

the torn leaves of Genesis,

    and a man covering himself

        with the Good Book's

    frontispiece — his own name

inscribed on the page.

knowlege & religion/morality

- learn nakedness ⟶ shame
  mortality
  child birth painful
  ⟶ pain of recognizing sin/shame

what do the white people
think makes them superior?

2 types of knowlege discovered
opposites/ ⎡ · bible/religion/writing makes
contradictory ⎣   superiority
      - they're no different (nakedness)

Taxonomy

After a series of casta *paintings by*
Juan Rodríguez Juárez, c. 1715

1. De Español y de India Produce Mestiso

The canvas is a leaden sky
    behind them, heavy
with words, gold letters inscribing
    an equation of blood —

this plus this equals this — as if
    a contract with nature, or
a museum label,
    ethnographic, precise. See

how the father's hand, beneath
    its crown of lace,
curls around his daughter's head;
    she's nearly fair

as he is — *calidad.* See it
    in the brooch at her collar,
the lace framing her face.
    An infant, she is borne

inhuman makes things mathematical

over the servant's left shoulder,
    bound to him
by a sling, the plain blue cloth
    knotted at his throat.

If the father, his hand
    on her skull, divines —
as the physiognomist does —
    the mysteries

child is valued

of her character, discursive,
    legible on her light flesh,
in the soft curl of her hair,
    we cannot know it: so gentle

the eye he turns toward her.
    The mother, glancing
sideways toward him —
    the scarf on her head

white as his face,

  his powdered wig — gestures

with one hand a shape

  like the letter C. *See,*

she seems to say,

  what we have made.

The servant, still a child, cranes

  his neck, turns his face

up toward all of them. He is dark

  as history, origin of the word

native: the weight of blood,

  a pale mistress on his back,

heavier every year.

2. DE ESPAÑOL Y NEGRA PRODUCE MULATO

Still, the centuries have not dulled
the sullenness of the child's expression.

If there is light inside him, it does not shine
through the paint that holds his face

in profile — his domed forehead, eyes
nearly closed beneath a heavy brow.

Though inside, the boy's father stands
in his cloak and hat. It's as if he's just come in,

or that he's leaving. We see him
transient, rolling a cigarette, myopic —

his eyelids drawn against the child
passing before him. At the stove,

mother & father seperate

only unified couples white?

the boy's mother contorts, watchful,
her neck twisting on its spine, red beads

yoked at her throat like a necklace of blood,
her face so black she nearly disappears

into the canvas, the dark wall upon which
we see the words that name them.

What should we make of any of this?
Remove the words above their heads,

put something else in place of the child —
a table, perhaps, upon which the man might set

his hat, or a dog upon which to bestow
the blessing of his touch — and the story

[handwritten marginal note, read bottom to top:] child symbol of combined oppression of parents

changes. The boy is a palimpsest of paint —
layers of color, history rendering him

that precise shade of in-between.
Before this he was nothing: blank

is nothing w/ out rank in society

canvas — before image or word, before
a last brush stroke fixed him in his place.

rank = whole identity

3. *De Español y Mestiza Produce Castiza*

How not to see
    in this gesture

the mind
    of the colony?

In the mother's arms,
    the child, hinged

at her womb —
    dark cradle

of mixed blood
    (call it *Mexico*) —

turns toward the father,
    reaching to him

as if back to Spain,
    to the promise of blood

alchemy — three easy steps
    to purity:

from a Spaniard and an Indian,
    a mestizo;

from a mestizo and a Spaniard,
    a castizo;

from a castizo and a Spaniard,
    a Spaniard.

We see her here —
    one generation away —

nearly slipping
    her mother's careful grip.

*rules of old world
not working in new
must create new hierarchy*

4. *THE BOOK OF CASTAS*

Call it the catalog
    of mixed bloods, or   *renamed*

book of nothing

    the book of naught:
        not Spaniard, not white, but

mulatto-returning-backwards (or
    hold-yourself-in-midair) and

    the *morisca*, the *lobo*, the *chino*,
        sambo, *albino*, and

the *no-te-entiendo* — the
    I don't understand you.

    Guidebook to the colony,
        record of each crossed birth,

it is the typology of taint,
    of stain: blemish: sullying spot:

that which can be purified,

    that which cannot — Canaan's

black fate. How like a dirty joke

    it seems: *what do you call*

    that space between

        the dark geographies of sex?

Call it the *taint* — as in

    T'aint one and t'aint the other —

    illicit and yet naming still

        what is between. Between

her parents, the child,

    mulatto-returning-backwards,

    cannot slip their hold,

        the triptych their bodies make

in paint, in blood: her name
  written down in the *Book*

  of Castas — all her kind
    in thrall to a word.

Kitchen Maid with Supper at Emmaus; or, The Mulata

After the painting by Diego Velázquez, c. 1619

She is the vessels on the table before her:
the copper pot tipped toward us, the white pitcher
clutched in her hand, the black one edged in red
and upside-down. Bent over, she is the mortar,
and the pestle at rest in the mortar — still angled
in its posture of use. She is the stack of bowls
and the bulb of garlic beside it, the basket hung
by a nail on the wall and the white cloth bundled
in it, the rag in the foreground recalling her hand.
She's the stain on the wall the size of her shadow —
the color of blood, the shape of a thumb. She is echo
of Jesus at table, framed in the scene behind her:
his white corona, her white cap. Listening, she leans
into what she knows. Light falls on half her face.

[handwritten margin notes: "identity comes from the objects she uses?" and "she changes identity to suit her task?"]

27

Knowledge

After a chalk drawing by J. H. Hasselhorst, 1864

Whoever she was, she comes to us like this:

    lips parted, long hair spilling from the table

like water from a pitcher, nipples drawn out

    for inspection. Perhaps to foreshadow

the object she'll become: a skeleton on a pedestal,

    a row of skulls on a shelf. To make a study

of the ideal female body, four men gather around her.

    She is young and beautiful and drowned —

a Venus de' Medici, risen from the sea, sleeping.

    As if we could mistake this work for sacrilege,

the artist entombs her body in a pyramid

    of light, a temple of science over which

the anatomist presides. In the service of beauty —

    to know it — he lifts a flap of skin

knowlege is science rather than religion here

beneath her breast as one might draw back a sheet.

    We will not see his step-by-step parsing,

woman objectified

a translation: *Mary* or *Katherine* or *Elizabeth*

    to *corpus, areola, vulva.* In his hands

loses humanity

instruments of the empirical — scalpel, pincers —

    cold as the room must be cold: all the men

in coats, trimmed in velvet or fur — soft as the down

    of her pubis. Now one man is smoking, another

tilts his head to get a better look. Yet another,

    at the head of the table, peers down as if

enthralled, his fist on a stack of books.

    In the drawing this is only the first cut,

she becomes woman?

a delicate wounding: and yet how easily

    the anatomist's blade opens a place in <u>me</u>,

29

like a curtain drawn upon a room in which

    each learned man is my father

father is disecting her?

and I hear, again, his words — *I study*

    my crossbreed child — misnomer

and taxonomy, the language of zoology. Here,

    he is all of them: the preoccupied man —

an artist, collector of experience; the skeptic angling

    his head, his thoughts tilting toward

what I cannot know; the marshaller of knowledge,

    knuckling down a stack of books; even

father

the dissector — his scalpel in hand like a pen

    poised above me, aimed straight for my heart.

The Americans ❧

1. DR. SAMUEL ADOLPHUS CARTWRIGHT ON DISSECTING THE WHITE NEGRO, 1851

To strip from the flesh

    the specious skin; to weigh

        in the brainpan

    seeds of white

pepper; to find in the body

    its own diminishment—

        blood-deep

    and definite; to measure the heft

of lack; to make of the work of faith

    the work of science, evidence

        the word of God: Canaan

be the *servant of servants;* thus

    to know the truth

        of this: (this derelict

corpus, a dark compendium, this

    atavistic assemblage—flatter

feet, bowed legs, a shorter neck) so

    deep the tincture

        —see it!—

we still know white from not.

2. *Blood*

After George Fuller's The Quadroon, *1880*

It must be the gaze of a benevolent viewer
upon her, framed as she is in the painting's
romantic glow, her melancholic beauty
meant to show the pathos of her condition:
black blood — that she cannot transcend it.
In the foreground she is shown at rest, seated,
her basket empty and overturned beside her
as though she would cast down the drudgery
to which she was born. A gleaner, hopeless
undine — the bucolic backdrop a dim aura
around her — she looks out toward us as if
to bridge the distance between. *Mezzo,*
intermediate, how different she's rendered
from the dark kin working the fields behind her.
If not for the ray of light appearing as if from beyond
the canvas, we might miss them — three figures
in the near distance, small as afterthought.

3. HELP, 1968

After a photograph from The Americans *by Robert Frank*

When I see Frank's photograph

of a white infant in the dark arms

of a woman who must be the maid,

I think of my mother and the year

we spent alone — my father at sea.

The woman stands in profile, back

against a wall, holding her charge,

their faces side by side — the look

on the child's face strangely prescient,

a tiny furrow in the space

between her brows. Neither of them

looks toward the camera; nor

do they look at each other. That year,

when my mother took me for walks,

she was mistaken again and again

for my maid. Years later she told me

she'd say I was her daughter, and each time
strangers would stare in disbelief, then
empty the change from their pockets. Now

I think of the betrayals of flesh, how
she must have tried to make of her face
an inscrutable mask and hold it there
as they made their small offerings —
pressing coins into my hands. How
like the woman in the photograph
she must have seemed, carrying me
each day — white in her arms — as if
she were a prop: a black backdrop,
the dark foil in this American story.

Mano Prieta

The green drapery is like a sheet of water
        behind us — a cascade in the backdrop
of the photograph, a rushing current

that would scatter us, carry us each
        away. This is 1969 and I am three —
still light enough to be nearly the color

of my father. His armchair is a throne
        and I am leaning into him, propped
against his knees — his hand draped

across my shoulder. On the chair's arm
        my mother looms above me,
perched at the edge as though

she would fall off. The camera records
        her single gesture. Perhaps to still me,
she presses my arm with a forefinger,

makes visible a hypothesis of blood,

    its empire of words: the imprint

on my body of her lovely dark hand.

De Español y Negra; Mulata

After the painting by Miguel Cabrera, c. 1763

What holds me first is the stemmed fruit

in the child's small hand, center

of the painting, then the word nearby: *Texocotes,*

a tiny inscription on the mother's basket —

vessel from which, the scene suggests, the fruit

has been plucked. Read: *exotic bounty*

of the new world — basket, fruit; womb, child.

And still, what looks to be

tenderness: the father caressing

his daughter's cheek, the painter's light

finding him — his profile glowing as if

lit beneath the skin. Then, the dominion

of his touch: with one hand he holds

the long stem gingerly, pressing it

against her face — his gesture at once

possessing both. Flanked by her parents,

the child, in half-light, looks out as if

    toward you, her left arm disappearing

behind her mother's cloak. Such contrast —

    how not to see it? — in the lush depths

of paint: the mother's flat outline,

    the black cloak making her blacker still,

the moon-white crescent of her eye

    the only light in her face. In the foreground,

she gestures — a dark signal in the air —

    her body advancing toward them

like spilled ink spreading on a page,

    a great pendulum eclipsing the light.

Mythology

1. *NOSTOS*

Here is the dark night
of childhood — flickering

lamplight, odd shadows
on the walls — giant and flame

projected through the clear
frame of my father's voice.

Here is the past come back
as metaphor: my father, as if

to ease me into sleep, reciting
the trials of Odysseus. Always

he begins with the Cyclops,
light at the cave's mouth

bright as knowledge, the pilgrim
honing a pencil-sharp stake.

2. QUESTIONS POSED BY THE DREAM

It's the old place on Jefferson Street
I've entered, a girl again, the house dark
and everyone sleeping — so quiet it seems

I'm alone. What can this mean now, more
than thirty years gone, to find myself
at the beginning of that long hallway

knowing, as I did then, what stands
at the other end? And why does the past
come back like this: looming, a human figure

formed — as if it had risen from the Gulf
— of the crushed shells that paved
our driveway, a sharp-edged creature

that could be conjured only by longing?
Why is it here blocking the dark passage
to my father's bookshelves, his many books?

3. *SIREN*

In this dream I am driving
a car, strapped to my seat

like Odysseus to the mast,
my father calling to me

from the back — luring me
to a past that never was. This

is the treachery of nostalgia.
This is the moment before

a ship could crash onto the rocks,
the car's back wheels tip over

a cliff. Steering, I must be
the crew, my ears deaf

to the sound of my father's voice;
I must be the captive listener

cleaving to his words. I must be
singing this song to myself.

Geography

1.

At the bottom of the exit ramp
my father waits for us, one foot
on the curb, right hand hooked
in the front pocket of his jeans,
a stack of books beneath his arm.
It's 1971, the last year we're still
together. My mother and I travel
this road, each week, to meet him—
I-10 from Mississippi to New Orleans—
and each time we pull off the highway
I see my father like this: raising his thumb
to feign hitchhiking—a stranger
passing through to somewhere else.

2.

At Wolf River my father is singing.
The sun is shining and there's a cooler
of Pabst in the shade. He is singing
and playing the guitar — the sad songs
I hide from each time: a man pining
for Irene or Clementine, a woman dead
on a slab at Saint James. I'm too young to know
this is foreshadowing. To get away from
the blues I don't understand, I wade in water
shallow enough to cross. On the bank
at the other side, I look back at him as if
across the years: he's smaller, his voice
lost in the distance between us.

3.

On the Gulf and Ship Island Line
my father and I walk the rails south
toward town. More than twenty years
gone, he's come back to see this place,
recollect what he's lost. What he recalls
of my childhood is here. We find it
in the brambles of blackberry, the coins
flattened on the tracks. We can't help it —
already, we're leaning too hard
toward metaphor: my father searching
for the railroad switch. *It was here, right
here,* he says, turning this way and that —
the rails vibrating now, a train coming.

Torna Atrás

After De Albina y Español, Nace Torna Atrás (From Albino
and Spaniard, a Return-Backwards Is Born), *anonymous,*
c. 1785–1790

The unknown artist has rendered the father a painter and so

we see him at his work: painting a portrait of his wife —

their dark child watching nearby, a servant grinding colors

in the corner. The woman poses just beyond his canvas

and cannot see her likeness, her less than mirror image

coming to life beneath his hand. He has rendered her

homely, so unlike the woman we see in this scene, dressed

in late-century fashion, a *chiqueador* — mark of beauty

in the shape of a crescent moon — affixed to her temple.

If I say his painting is unfinished, that he has yet to make her

beautiful, to match the elegant sweep of her hair,

the graceful tilt of her head, has yet to adorn her dress

with lace and trim, it is only one way to see it. You might see,

instead, that the artist — perhaps to show his own skill —

has made the father a dilettante, incapable of capturing

his wife's beauty. Or, that he cannot see it: his mind's eye

reducing her to what he's made as if to reveal the illusion

immanent in her flesh. If you consider the century's mythology

of the body — that a dark spot marked the genitals of anyone with African blood — you might see how the black moon

on her white face recalls it: the *roseta* she passes to her child

marking him *torna atrás*. If I tell you such terms were born

in the Enlightenment's hallowed rooms, that the wages of empire

is myopia, you might see the father's vision as desire embodied

in paint, this rendering of his wife born of need to see himself

as architect of Truth, benevolent patriarch, father of uplift

ordering his domain. And you might see why, to understand

my father, I look again and again at this painting: how it is

that a man could love — and so diminish what he loves.

Bird in the House

A gift, you said, when we found it.
    And because my mother was dead,

I thought the cat had left it for me. The bird
    was black as omen, like a single crow

meaning sorrow. It was the year
    you'd remarried, summer —

the fields high and the pond reflecting
    everything: the willow, the small dock,

the crow overhead that — doubled —
    should have been an omen for joy.

Forgive me, Father, that I brought to that house
    my grief. You will not recall telling me

you could not understand my loss, not until
    your own mother died. Each night I'd wake

from a dream, my heart battering my rib cage —
    a trapped, wild bird. I did not know then

the cat had brought in a second grief: what was it
    but animal knowledge? Forgive me

that I searched for meaning in everything
    you did, that I watched you bury the bird

in the backyard — your back to me; I saw you
    flatten the mound, erasing it into the dirt.

Artifact

As long as I can remember you kept the rifle —
    your grandfather's, *an antique* you called it —

in your study, propped against the tall shelves
    that held your many books. Upright,

beside those hard-worn spines, it was another
    backbone of your past, a remnant I studied

as if it might unlock — like the skeleton key
    its long body resembled — some door I had yet

to find. Peering into the dark muzzle, I imagined a bullet
    as you described: spiraling through the bore

and spinning straight for its target. It did not hit me
    then: the rifle I'd inherit showing me

how one life is bound to another, that hardship
    endures. For years I admired its slender profile,

until — late one night, somber with drink — you told me
    it still worked, that you kept it loaded *just in case,*

and I saw the rifle for what it is: a relic
    sharp as sorrow, the barrel hollow as regret.

Fouled

From the next room I hear my father's voice,
a groan at first, a sound so sad I think he must be
reliving a catalog of things lost: all the dead
come back to stand ringside, the glorious body
of his youth — a light heavyweight, fight-ready
and glistening — that beauty I see now in pictures.
Looking into the room, I half imagine I'll find him
shadowboxing the dark, arms and legs twitching
as a dog runs in sleep. Tonight, I've had to help him
into bed — stumbling up the stairs, his arm a weight
on my shoulders so heavy it nearly brought us down.
Now his distress cracks open the night; he is calling
my name. I could wake him, tell him it's only a dream,
that I am *here*. Here is the threshold I do not cross:
a sliver of light through the doorway finds his tattoo,
the anchor on his forearm tangled in its chain.

Rotation

Like the moon that night, my father —
　　a distant body, white and luminous.
How small I was back then,
　　looking up as if from dark earth.

Distant, his body white and luminous,
　　my father stood in the doorway.
Looking up as if from dark earth,
　　I saw him outlined in a scrim of light.

My father stood in the doorway
　　as if to watch over me as I dreamed.
When I saw him outlined — a scrim of light —
　　he was already waning, turning to go.

Once, he watched over me as I dreamed.
　　How small I was. Back then,
he was already turning to go, waning
　　like the moon that night — my father.

Thrall

Juan de Pareja, 1670

He was not my father
though   he might have been
    I came to him
the mulatto son
       of a slave woman
    just that
as if   it took only my mother
    to make me
      a *mulatto*
meaning
       any white man
could be my father

    ❖

In his shop   bound
    to the muller
I ground his colors
      my hands dusted   black
with fired bone   stained
      blue   and flecked
with glass   my nails
edged vermilion   as if

              my fingertips bled
In this way   just as
        I'd turned the pages
of his books
        I meant to touch
                everything he did

        ❖

With Velázquez   in Rome
        a divination
At market   I lingered to touch
        the bright hulls of lemons
                closed my eyes until
        the scent was oil
and thinner   yellow ocher
        in my head
                And once
the sudden taste of iron
                a glimpse of red
        like a wound opening
                the robes of the pope
at portrait

       that bright shade of blood

          before it darkens

purpling nearly to black

     ❖

Because he said

       painting was not

       labor   was

the province of free men

       I could only

watch   Such beauty

       in the work of his hands

          his quick strokes

       a divine language I learned

over his shoulder

       my own hands

tracing the air

       in his wake   Forbidden

          to answer in paint

I kept my canvases secret

       hidden until

       Velázquez decreed

unto me

myself   Free

I was apprentice   he

my master still

❖

How intently at times

could he fix his keen eye

upon me

though only once

did he fix me   in paint

my color a study

my eyes wide

as I faced him

a lace collar at my shoulders

as though I'd been born

noble

the yoke of my birth

gone from my neck

In his hand   a long brush

to keep him far

from the canvas

far from it   as I was

    the distance between us

       doubled   that

he could observe me

    twice   stand closer

       to what *he* made

For years   I looked to it

    as one looks into a mirror

    ❖

    And so

in *The Calling of Saint Matthew*

    I painted my own

likeness   a freeman

    in the House of Customs

       waiting to pay

my duty   In my hand

    an answer   a slip of paper

       my signature on it

    Juan de Pareja   1661

Velázquez   one year gone

    Behind me

upright on a shelf

a forged platter   luminous

as an aureole

just beyond my head

my face turned

to look out from the scene

a self-portrait

To make it

I looked at how

my master saw me   then

I narrowed my eyes

❖

Now

at the bright edge

of sleep   *mother*

She comes back to me

as sound

her voice

in the echo of birdcall

a single syllable

again

and again   my name
        Juan Juan Juan
or   a bit of song   that
            waking
I cannot grasp

Calling

Mexico, 1969

Why not make a fiction

      of the mind's fictions? I want to say

   it begins like this: the trip

      a pilgrimage, my mother

kneeling at the altar of the Black Virgin,

      enthralled — light streaming in

     a window, the sun

    at her back, holy water

   in a bowl she must have touched.

What's left is palimpsest — one memory

     bleeding into another, overwriting it.

      How else to explain

       what remains? The sound

  of water in a basin I know is white,

     the sun behind her, light streaming in,

     her face —

as if she were already dead — blurred

    as it will become.

I want to imagine her before

the altar, rising to meet us, my father

lifting me

toward her outstretched arms.

What else to make

of the mind's slick confabulations?

What comes back

is the sun's dazzle on a pool's surface,

light filtered through water

closing over my head, my mother — her body

between me and the high sun, a corona of light

around her face. Why not call it

a vision? What I know is this:

I was drowning and saw a dark Madonna;

someone pulled me through

the water's bright ceiling

and I rose, initiate,

from one life into another.

Enlightenment ☙

In the portrait of Jefferson that hangs

    at Monticello, he is rendered two-toned:

his forehead white with illumination —

a lit bulb — the rest of his face in shadow,

    darkened as if the artist meant to contrast

his bright knowledge, its dark subtext.

By 1805, when Jefferson sat for the portrait,

    he was already linked to an affair

with his slave. Against a backdrop, blue

and ethereal, a wash of paint that seems

    to hold him in relief, Jefferson gazes out

across the centuries, his lips fixed as if

he's just uttered some final word.

    The first time I saw the painting, I listened

as my father explained the contradictions:

how Jefferson hated slavery, though — *out*

   of necessity, my father said — had to own

slaves; that his moral philosophy meant

he could not have fathered those children:

   would have been impossible, my father said.

For years we debated the distance between

word and deed. I'd follow my father from book

   to book, gathering citations, listen

as he named — like a field guide to Virginia —

each flower and tree and bird as if to prove

   a man's pursuit of knowledge is greater

than his shortcomings, the limits of his vision.

I did not know then the subtext

   of our story, that my father could imagine

Jefferson's words made flesh in my flesh —

the improvement of the blacks in body

  and mind, in the first instance of their mixture

with the whites — or that my father could believe

he'd made me *better*. When I think of this now,

  I see how the past holds us captive,

its beautiful ruin etched on the mind's eye:

my young father, a rough outline of the old man

  he's become, needing to show me

the better measure of his heart, an equation

writ large at Monticello. That was years ago.

  Now, we take in how much has changed:

talk of Sally Hemings, someone asking,

How white was she? — parsing the fractions

  as if to name what made her worthy

of Jefferson's attentions: a near-white,

quadroon mistress, not a plain black slave.

Imagine stepping back into the past,
our guide tells us then — and I can't resist

whispering to my father: *This is where*
we split up. I'll head around to the back.
When he laughs, I know he's grateful

I've made a joke of it, this history
that links us — white father, black daughter —
even as it renders us other to each other.

How the Past Comes Back

Like shadow across a stone,
    gradually —
        the name it darkens;

as one enters the world
        through language —
    like a child learning to speak
      then naming
everything; as *flower,*

the neglected hydrangea
        endlessly blossoming —
      year after year
    each bloom a blue refrain; as

the syllables of birdcall
    coalescing in the trees,
      repeating
a single word:
    forgets;

as the dead bird's bright signature —

      days after you buried it —

   a single red feather

      on the window glass

in the middle of your reflection.

On Happiness

To see a flash of silver —
     pale undersides of the maple leaves
catching light — quick movement
     at the edge of thought,
          is to be pulled back
to that morning, to the river where it flashes still:
           a single fish
breaking the water's surface,
     the almost-caught taunting our lines
          until we give up, at last, and turn
the boat toward home; is
     to see it clearly: the salmon
          rolling, showing me
a glimpse of the unattainable — happiness
     I would give my father if I could;
          and then is to recall the permit
he paid for that morning, see it
     creased in my back pocket — how
he'd handed it to me
     and I'd tucked it there, as if
          a guarantee.

Vespertina Cognitio

> . . . the knowledge of man is an evening knowledge . . .
> — *Ralph Waldo Emerson,* Nature

Overhead, pelicans glide in threes —

  their shadows across the sand

    dark thoughts crossing the mind.

Beyond the fringe of coast, shrimpers

  hoist their nets, weighing the harvest

    against the day's losses. Light waning,

concentration is a lone gull

  circling what's thrown back. Debris

    weights the trawl like stones.

All day, this dredging — beneath the tug

  of waves: rhythm of what goes out,

    comes back, comes back, comes back.

Illumination ●

Always   there is something more to know
      what lingers   at the edge of thought
awaiting illumination   as in
      this secondhand book   full
of annotations   daring the margins in pencil
a light stroke as if
      the writer of these small replies
meant not to leave them   forever
      meant to erase
evidence of this private interaction
      Here   a passage underlined   there
a single star on the page
      as in a night sky   cloud-swept and hazy
where only the brightest appears
      a tiny spark   I follow
its coded message   try to read in it
the direction of the solitary mind
      that thought to pencil in
a jagged arrow   It
      is a bolt of lightning

where it strikes

    I read the line over and over

as if I might discern

    the little fires set

the flames of an idea   licking the page

how knowledge burns   Beyond

    the exclamation point

its thin agreement   angle of surprise

there are questions   the word *why*

So much is left

    untold   Between

the printed words   and the self-conscious scrawl

    between   what is said and not

white space framing the story

    the way the past   unwritten

eludes us   So much

    is implication   the afterimage

of measured syntax   always there

    ghosting the margins that words

their black-lined authority

do not cross   Even

as they rise up   to meet us

the white page hovers beneath

silent   incendiary   waiting

Notes

"Miracle of the Black Leg"

The texts and images referred to in the poem are discussed in *The Phantom Limb Phenomenon: A Medical, Folkloric, and Historical Study, Texts and Translations of Tenth- to Twentieth-Century Accounts of the Miraculous Restoration of Lost Body Parts,* by Douglas B. Price, M.D., and Neil J. Twombly, S.J., Ph.D. (Georgetown University Press, 1978), and in *One Leg in the Grave: The Miracle of the Transplantation of the Black Leg by the Saints Cosmas and Damian,* by Kees W. Zimmerman (The Netherlands: Elsevier/Bunge, 1998). Representations of the myth appear in Greek narratives, in a Scottish poem, and in paintings and altarpieces in Spain, Italy, Germany, Austria, Portugal, Switzerland, France, and Belgium.

"Taxonomy"

Casta paintings illustrated the various mixed unions of colonial Mexico and the children of those unions whose names and taxonomies were recorded in the *Book of Castas.* The widespread belief in the "taint" of black blood — that it was irreversible — resulted in taxonomies rooted in language that implied a "return backwards." From *Casta Painting: Images of Race in Eighteenth-Century Mexico,* by Ilona Katzew (New Haven: Yale University Press, 2004).

"Mano Prieta"

The term *mano prieta* (dark hand) "refers to mestizos, coyotes, mulattos, lobos, zambiagos, moriscos." From *Descripción del Estado político de la Nueva España,* anonymous, 1735; quoted in *Casta Painting: Images of Race in Eighteenth-Century Mexico,* by Ilona Katzew (New Haven: Yale University Press, 2004).

"Thrall"

Juan de Pareja (1606–1670) was the slave of the artist Diego Velázquez until his manumission in 1650. For many years Pareja served Velázquez as a laborer in his studio and later sat for the portrait *Juan de Pareja,* which Velázquez painted in order to practice for creating a portrait of Pope Innocent X. Pareja was also a painter and is best known for his work *The Calling of Saint Matthew.* From *El Museo pictórico y escala óptica,* volume 3, by Antonio Palomino (Madrid, 1947, p. 913; this volume was originally published in 1724).

Acknowledgments

Many thanks to the editors of the following journals in which these poems, sometimes in different versions, first appeared: *Callaloo*, "*Kitchen Maid with Supper at Emmaus; or, The Mulata*" and "*Mano Prieta*"; *Cave Wall*, "Bird in the House"; *Charlotte: Journal of Literature and Art*, "The Americans (2. Blood)"; *Chattahoochee Review*, "How the Past Comes Back" and "*Torna Atrás*"; *Connotation Press: An Online Artifact*, "Fouled"; *Ecotone*, "On Happiness" and "Thrall"; *Five Points*, "Geography," "On Captivity," and "Rotation"; *Fugue*, "Illumination" (as "Afterimage"); *Georgia Review*, "Mythology"; *Green Mountains Review*, "Artifact"; *Gulf Coast*, "Taxonomy (3. *De Español y Mestiza Produce Castiza* and 4. *The Book of Castas*)"; *Hollins Critic*, "The Americans (3. Help, 1968)"; *New England Review*, "Knowledge," "Elegy," and "The Americans (1. Dr. Samuel Adolphus Cartwright on Dissecting the White Negro, 1851)," and "Taxonomy (2. De Español y Negra Produce Mulato)"; *Ploughshares*, "Taxonomy (1. *De Español y de India Produce Mestiso*)"; *Poetry Northwest*, "*De Español y Negra; Mulata*" and "Calling" (as "Mexico"); *Tin House*, "Miracle of the Black Leg"; Virginia Quarterly Review, "Enlightenment"; *Waccamaw*, "*Vespertina Cognitio.*"

"On Captivity" also appeared in *American Poet*, Fall 2008, and in *Best American Poetry 2008*, edited by Charles Wright and David Lehman. "Elegy" also appeared in *Best American Poetry 2011*, edited by Kevin Young and David Lehman. "The Americans (1. Dr. Samuel Adolphus Cartwright on Dissecting the White Negro, 1851)" will appear in *Best American Poetry 2012*, edited by Mark Doty and David Lehman. *Best American Poetry* is published annually by Scribner.

My gratitude as well to the Emory University Research Committee and to the Beinecke Rare Book and Manuscript Library and the Department of African American Studies at Yale University for fellowships that allowed me time to complete this book. For their thoughtful comments and support, I am indebted to Elizabeth Alexander, Claudia Emerson, Ben George, Shara McCallum, Rob McQuilkin, Rhett Trull, C. Dale Young, Kevin Young, and — most of all — Michael Collier. To Brett Gadsden, my deepest thanks.